MY LIFE SONG

Barbara,

Happy Journeying.

Sandy.

MY LIFE SONG
A JOURNEY BACK TO ME

Sandra F. Dexter

©2021, Sandra F. Dexter
Printed in the United States of America
26 25 24 23 22 21   1 2 3 4 5

ISBN 978-0-9991218-4-9

Book design & production by Marjorie DeLuca
Aspen Graphic Solutions · info@aspengfx.com
Cover photo by Barbara S. Reese, ©2021

Preface

I'm pleased to be able to share my journey with you
through poetry.

These poems are printed in chronological order
to show the peaks and valleys of my journey.
Perhaps some will resonate with you.

The poems came to me in many ways,
from dreams, while walking,
through prompts at workshops,
while journaling, and more.

The section titles are the years in which
the poems were written, not the year in which
events may have occurred.

Contents

2012

Dedication

This book is dedicated to the 4-year-old
wearing a white dress and red boots,
high stepping to her equine friend, Sweetfire.

Sometimes you need a new pair of boots
when you embark on a new journey.

SANDRA F. DEXTER

Walking in My Power

Red boots
Up to my knees
Red boots
If you please
Red boots
I stand so tall
Red boots
I'm through the wall
Red boots
See me fly
Red boots
Up so high
Red boots
I'm in my power
Red boots
With Sweetfire
Red boots
We're both so strong
Red boots
We can't go wrong
Red boots
We have such fun
Red boots

We're on the run

Red boots

Come dance with me

Red boots

They set me free

Red boots

My heart's afire

Red boots

My heart's desire

Red boots

2009

My Life Song

The fairies dance
On wings of delight
They entice me to play
To let in the light

I'm the drummer, the dancer
Calling angels and spirits
To join in my song
My Life Song

I'm back in the chrysalis
Preparing to fly
Painting the picture
Of my life

I go back in to the gray
To find the gift
To find the good in me
I dig through the terror and the pain
To find my strength
To embrace all parts of me
To release the fear
To release the pain

I call on the magic
That lies there within
To help me forgive, to help me see
To let out the light
That resides in me
To let out the light
That resides in me

I Found My Voice

I found my voice
I found my voice
It was buried deep within
Was not easy
To dig it out
But worth the
Journey in

Joy in My Soul

There is joy
Deep in my soul
There is joy
That makes me whole
There is joy
Let it spread out
To every cell
Let it shout
I am God
I am Peace
I am Love
I am Light
Let my soul
Shine so bright
That it glows in the night.

The Thaw

Springtime
Lying in the grass
My beautiful back yard
Now
Feeling the warmth of the sun
And the still cool air
And then
April showers
Bring May flowers
I always liked that

April, my favorite month
The month of my birth
Snow melting, ice melting
Then Minnesota, now Colorado

Seems like March always came in like a lamb
        and went out like a lion
And the groundhog always saw its shadow
Meaning six more weeks of winter

But April, the brightness of April
Longer days

Warmer days
More sunshine, more light

Hard to remember back then
Walking around the puddles
After an April shower
The air so fresh, never fresher
Just warm, jacket weather
The thaw
The true thaw
The final thaw
After a long cold winter

Is this April to be my thaw
After the long cold winter of held-to traumas?
Is this the final thaw
The true letting go
Breaking out of the cocoon
Finally taking flight
Into the light
Free at last
To be me
To live me

What to Write

I sit to write
But the words
Don't come
I long to write
But the words
Don't come
So I write
I write
I write
I write
I write
And I write
The words
I write.

I write,
"What to write,
What to write,
What to write,
What to write,"
Just write
Any word that comes to mind,
The words,

I write

Come to mind

Write now,

So I write

I write

And see what comes out.

I go in

I open the channel

The flow just begins

I look in the wellspring

Of my heart.

It seems hollow

Just empty to me.

How can that be?

No words in there

No feelings, too.

Just what's in there?

What do I do?

An empty well

That's what I am.

No more words

No more words

They don't come

Are they buried so deep

Hidden from view
That I can't see them
Nor can you?
How do I find them?
Where do I look?
That can't be all
The words I took.
I wrote of pain
I wrote of sorrow
Of finding joy and love
I wrote of release and letting go
Now how do I write
Of me?
I'm whole.
Are there no words?
Am I empty?
I'm painting the picture
Of my life.
Where are the words
To write
This life?
What do I want
This life to be?
I want to write,
Abundantly.

Where are the words?
Don't stop the flow
Keep writing
Keep writing
Any words
Write now
Just write
Just write
Just write
You'll see
The words will come
Eventually.
Don't give it up.
Don't stop now.
You've come so far
Just let it out.
No more struggle
No more strife
With ease and grace
You'll paint your life.
Keep it simple
Don't struggle, dear,
You've come home to God
Right here.

On this path
You'll find such joy
And love
Like you've never known.
So hang in there
Be patient, dear
The words will come
And you will hear
No more struggle
No more strife
Let God be the driver
In your life.
Each day is new
To re-create
Don't worry about
Any mistakes
They can be undone
Just start afresh
Each day.

When you are blue
You know what to do
Just sit and write
Take pen in hand.
Put it on the page

And let the words
Fall where they may.
Don't worry if
They're good or bad
No judging here
Just write
It will free up—
The block will go
The channel will open
For that free flow
Just write each word
As it comes up
Just write and write
And don't give up.
DETERMINATION!

Walk Me through This Life

God, walk me through this life
Keep me free from fear
Let the peace win out
That I hold so dear.

Master and Commander

I
Can demand
Without
The anger
Without
The emotional charge.

I
Can demand
Without
The violence.
It's called
Assertive
Not aggressive.

Maybe
It's command
Not demand.

The movie
Comes to mind,
Master and Commander.

He was
Master and commander
Of his ship.

I am
Master and commander
Of my life.

Grist

Grist for the mill.
Oil in my lamp.
Shining my light.
Being a beacon.
Being that light.

The Truth of Me

I come to this place
Of freedom now.
I've done the work
To get here.
Awareness,
That is the key
And God
In the driver's seat.

So help me move on
To grow and expand.
To be who I'm meant
To be.

There's nothing better
From where I stand
Than God
Living through me.

So I'll take my freedom
For that's where
My peace comes.
And I'll live

The Full Ness
Of life.

I'll share
And I'll care
Without all
The fear.

I'll hold fast
To the truth
Of me.

Gently

Take it easy
Take it slow
No need to rush
Breathe
Let the breath go.
Don't stop the breath
Don't block the breath
Pamper yourself
No more
Up on the shelf
Time to live
Time to experience
Gently
Gently

Take it easy
Take it slow
There's nowhere
To go
It's all right here
Where you stand

Take it easy

Take it slow
Take it easy
Take it slow
Gently
Gently
As you go
Through this life

Take it easy
Take it slow
There's no where
To go
It's all right here
Where you stand

Standing in your power
Standing for you
For yourself
No more
Up on the shelf
Being aware
Taking part
Living life
From your heart

Take it easy
Take it slow
There's no where to go
It's all right here
Where you stand

Stand for
What you believe in
Stand for your
Right
To be treated well
Stand for your right
For health and wealth
Radiant health
All kinds of wealth

Stand and demand
Kindly, respectfully
Stand and command
Kindly, respectfully

Radiant health
All kinds of wealth

Love and prosperity
God's love
Flowing through me
Gently
Gently

Gently
Gently

Take it easy
Take it slow
Take it easy
Take it slow
There's nowhere
To go
It's all right here
Where you stand.

Gently II

Gently
Gently
Into the night
The dark night of
The soul

Gently through
Back to you
God,
Back to you
Lift the gray
Dissolve it now,
Like the fog
Let the light
Shine through

Lift the fog
Dissolve it now
Let the light
Shine through

What to do?
What to do?
What to do?

Just move
Gently through
Dissipate the fog
Gently
Gently
Gently
Into the night
The dark night of
The Soul
For freedom
For light

Freedom, light, laughter.

2011

Passion

Where is my passion
I look around and see
Others have passion
But not me

I envy them
   their passion
For a hobby
   or a job

I look inside
   to find
My passion
   My zest
    for life

Where did it go
   Where can it
    be

My passion
   For life

For now
   I'll just take

one step at
a time

I'll come to my
passion
Somewhere along
the line

It will come
out
From inside
of me

And show
itself
so clearly
to me

I'll just be
patient
I'll wait and see
I'll find that
passion
Inside of
me.

Hooked

June 1994

Fish hooks dangling
What are those called
The treble hooks
The red and white ones
Hooked in my body,
So many of them
No pain, no feeling
Just there, dangling
One in my right eye
I tell the doctor,
"That's the only one I'm concerned about.
It doesn't hurt either,
But I don't see much out of the other eye, and
I'm worried this hook will mess up the vision
In my good eye."
The doctor says,
"Nothing to be concerned about."
"Ok."

June 2010

Years pass
Dixon Reservoir

Water to mid-calf
Fish hooks dangling at the ends of
Fishing line arcing out of my body.
Like Play-Doh pushing through holes
My mind thinks
This isn't the way they were in the dream
Wants to put them back
My fingers clip like scissors
Cutting
Hooks and lines fall away

June 2011
Fish hooks, fish hooks
In my head
Fish hooks, fish hooks
I can't rest

What are these hooks?
What do they mean?
Whooo's got their hooks
In me?

Punctuation

Punctuation
Or rather
Lack thereof.

What does that say?
No punctuation
In my life
Everything running
Together
No boundaries.
Like the hooks
In me.

Always Something

There's always something

Do this, clear that
Spew out the old,
The battered
Keeping the demons
At bay
Moving away
One step at a time
Into the void,
The unknown
For better or worse
'Til death do us part.

Loneliness

Lonely
Loneliness
   Aloneness
    Isolated
     Left out
      Left behind
       Don't belong
        Don't fit in
Solitude   Separated
      Separation

What is loneliness
   to me?
   Separation

Connect inside
   in order to
   connect
    outside

I must connect
   to me

Before I can
    connect
       to others

Connections
    Connections
    Connections

Loneliness
    Scary
      Frightening
        Dark places
          Dark places

Solitude

False Starts

I whack my toes
    and stumble
Through the current
    of life
False starts
    Cheesy
I regain my
    balance.

Memories

She's gathering them
    Books
Or rather
    Book covers
Different shapes and sizes,
    Colors, textures
Into one tall stack
    Some this direction
    Some that
Not squared up
In easy reach
    So she can pull them off
One at a time to
    Look at them.

Bedtime

Just another day
We went out to play.

A fabulous day.

Why do I feel so blue?

The fabulous day
    has come to an end
And it's bedtime.

Freak time.
Fright time
Sting time, cry time.
    Curl up and die time.

Leave me alone.
I want to go home.
I don't want to go home.

Both Worlds

Two ends of the pendulum
    Swing
Meet in the middle
Hold the same space
The pain of trauma
And the heart of love
What if I said
    I love you
To the pain
Between your heart
    and mine
One and the same.

Glorious Day

Oh, glorious day
We went out
    to play
Soap bubbles
    for our adventure
A picnic lunch
Then sitting by
    the river
Writing poetry
Laughing
    & talking
    & singing
    & dancing
Oh, joyous day
We get to play
    & play & play & play
Lots of play.

My Primordial Self

My primordial self is…

Hidden inside
Waiting to escape

It is…

The anger that erupts
The fear that paralyzes

It is…

The urge to scream
The nervous system gone awry

It is…

The beauty and the beast
The protector and inhibitor

It is…
    me.

My Original Face

is beauty.........at its best

is love.........unconditional

is worthiness.........without cause

is abundance.........from within

Twilight

Delicate, brittle bones
Being set aside
 Piece by piece
Ever so gently
Why didn't I keep them
 Intact?

Old, brittle memories
Die away
Disintegrate

A new day
 Dawns
A pale orange
Not as bright as
 Expected

2012

Stuck

The pain
The anguish
The frustration
   Wanting to cry
     Crying
      Holding it in
    Holding back.
    Exploding
    Freeing
All of it.
Write it.

Fuck you.
    I can't write it.

Pain wraps sides
    abdomen
      back.
Around and around
    gnawing
      eating away
    my innards.

How do I write these words?
    These thoughts?
    These sounds?
    What's around me?
    What's in me?

Melancholy

Powdery snow
　　Floats away
　　　on the air
　　　currents
　　　　of life

Melancholy
　　Apathy
　　　Waste of
　　　　time
Sitting here
　　Pretending, wanting
　　　To write
　　　　To draw.
　　　To create
　　　　What?
　　A poem—no words
　　　to combine.
　A picture
　　no lines
　　　to shine
　　　to define.

Nothing to
     express
Blank

And the pain shows up
     again
Wraps sides
     abdomen.
       back.

Morning Peace

Sitting at the table
Snow on the ground
Blue sky overhead

Cat in the tree
Bird on the wing
Life goes on

Feet fly
Wings flap
Silent inside

Trees and blue sky
Mountain edges cut the sky
Where am I?

Lost in thought
Clothes slapping in the dryer
The cat purrs

The Freeze

Turning in
    Closing up.
      Tuning out

Can't do nothin' but read.
    Takes me away
      Away from the pain
      The overwhelm.

Slide

Dark
    So dark

Now
    Slight lightening
        at the mountain top
    Gradual definition of
        tree limbs

And soon
    the ground.

Word Clouds

Sun, glorious sun
   Shine on me
     today

Bright sky
   Bird on the wing
     Snow on the ground.

Fill me up with
   Vitamin D.
     Lift my mood.

View of Sunlight peak
   Open me up
     Let me speak.

Of past & present &
   days
     to come

Of memories
   & dreams

Of what I wish
   my life
     to be.

Creating clouds
   to drift through
     my mind.

Reeling in
   what
     tickles my fancy

Bringing it home
   to my
     heart

Where it can
   grow
     and thrive

Word clouds
   What do you say
     to me
       today?

Drifting

Snowflakes drifting down
Gently
Each in its own space
Drawn to the ground.

Gone?

Soup du jour?
Beans & rice?
What do I eat?

Hold this body upright?
Grant me liberty?

What place would I be
If I broke down & bled?

Holes in my head?

Letting out the pain?
Flowing like a stream?

Gone, beneath the dream?

Melt

Sun on the mountain
Beneath the trees—shade.
Snow patches
    linger
Where the sun doesn't
      shine
Give me time
     And I'll melt
      the shade
     Of my life.
Like the snow in
      Spring.

Hidden

Deer in the trees
Hidden from view.

Just like my nights
Asleep at the wheel

Something flicks by
My peripheral view.

A bird on the wing.
Or…
     what could it be?

I don't want to see.

A Few Short Days

Green cactus butterfly
Wings spread
    against a backdrop of rock.
They tell me
    a butterfly survives
      a mere few days
        out of its chrysalis.

My wings
    grow sturdy
      like the leaves
        of the cactus
My time
    in the chrysalis
      and prior
        much longer than
          the caterpillar.
    Proportionally,
      a long-lived flight.

But would it matter
    were it not?
      Ohh, to spread my

Wings
And fly
If only for
a
few
short
days.

Mourning Dove

Bright yellow cowslips
 Leaves floating on swamp water
  Roots growing down
   Sun glinting through pines
    Behind Grandmother's house
   Mourning dove
   In Grandmother's yard
  Dimming light
  Not knowing where safety is
 Eyes darting through tall trees
4 year old petite

Note: This poem may be read in many directions, forward, backward, from the inside out or from the outside in.

Coming Soon to a Theater near You

Optimism

That bright light
  In my
    Mind's eye

That feeling of
  Everything's okay
  In my heart

That feeling good
  now
And looking forward
  to the future
A future blessed
  with light
    from
      within
        and
          from outside
          of me.

Expansive
   Bright
     Flight
  So much to see
   and to
    write.

Give Them Something

I come across her
alone
in a room
scared, ill,
very thin
a lightweight
insubstantial
feathers falling away as she
grooms them.
I think she won't
survive.

I pick her up
hold her against my heart
She calms
Feathers fluff, thicken
A now-substantial body
Comes to life
beneath soft, powdery
     blue and gray feathers.

She says,
"Please give Them something so

They don't have to remember about themselves
What I have to remember about myself.
There is something you can give them,
isn't there?"

I say, "Yes."

I set her down
gently, tell her,
"I will be back, there's something I
need to do."

I wake,
arms and shoulders achy,
heavy, weighted
down.

Hands puffy,
hot.

Over the Edge, Into the Abyss

I

The careless, carless man
Careening out of control

Curvy, windy, narrow,
Two-lane highway
Up, up,
The Man
Upright, feet inches above the ground
Me—
The passenger

He careens across the lanes
Catches the outside curve
We're over now
No
Back to center
Another outside curve
We're over

I watch him, suspended in midair, supine
I think, "This could be over in moments
Hitting the ground, splat, broken bones,

So quick, almost no pain."

Then I think,
"Time can speed up or slow down."
The slowing down gives me time to decide:
"I don't want to commit suicide."

I'm lifted from beneath
Raised to highway level
Don't know where I'll land.

II

A notebook binder
Dark beneath the teeth
Big spaces to climb inside
I think I should go in
Take a flashlight so I can see.

Trepidation

I

Rickety rungs
Nailed to a wall
Pulling away

I might fall backward

I push them back in
Climb down
Wait for them to be fixed
Before proceeding
To the attic.

II

The attic

I push up the
Trap door
Three dogs, in the way
Two big, one tiny
Not yet
I close the door
    On them.

Top of the ladder
Elbows pulling me up
I back down
Not ready, yet.

Jesus and Him

But it was more than the
   alcohol.
He was crazy evil.
The booze just brought that
   out.
Crazy, evil.

After I left
He sang Christian songs
   at the bar.
So I heard.
Talked how he found Christ.
Then came and beat me.
Preached to me
   over the phone.
Said, "It says
   in the Bible
Divorce is wrong."
But apparently not
   beating your wife.

That was okay
   by
      Jesus and him.

Duality

Curling up, curling in
Expansiveness
 Duality

My soul pushes out
My heart says
 No!
My soul retreats.

Open my heart, God
 Open my heart
For healing
 True healing
Comes
 with a heart that is open
 and a soul that is free.

Inch by Inch

Daylight breaks
A new dawn
rises
Bright with
possibilities

Slowly, slowly
Inch by inch
Releasing the old
Welcoming the new

A new day
A new life
Ripe with possibilities
Welcoming them in
Inch by inch by inch

No Joke

Just as words
   come.
One by one.

Send them back
   for a
      long joke.

Don't pester me
   now
I'm tired.

Tired of life
Tired of the struggle

To free myself

Let me rest
Take a break

Come back
   to it
      later.

A long rest—no joke.

Saturn

Hope,
Once easy and clear
Became marred
With the blood of trauma.

Bang my door
Eat my flesh
I should be doing
Exactly what I'm doing.

I showcase in
You come out
Where does the trauma
    end?

Saturn is lost
The beautiful rings
How do I find them
back?

Fruit of the Soul

Plant the seeds
In fertile soil
Where they can grow
Rich and strong.

My seeds
Seeds of love
Seeds of joy
Seeds of peace.

Find the rich, black
    Loam
And plant them
    There.

Water them
Nourish them
Watch them grow
And expand.

See them blossom
And bear fruit
The fruit of your
    Soul.

2013

Help

I

A river flows
Past her teenage home
Where the county road once ran.

She
Partially submerged
Upright
Stepping backward
From stone to stone

Changing direction
She notices
    submerged boulders
And the swiftness
    of the current

A man to her left
Arm reaching

II

She floats up the stairs

Behind those carrying the body
Wrapped like a mummy in warm blankets
She watches them lie her on the bed

The man from the river
Beside her
Says
You need to stay here
You can't leave.

III

Three kids
Each standing on their own paddleboard
Backs straight
Legs spread
Surrounding the board that carries
The mummy wrapped body

She hovers
Above the river where earlier
the water flowed round her
She watches
As the river carries them
    downstream.

She thinks,
They can't stay upright
when they hit rough water.
She wonders
How far away is help and
will they get there in time.

The man
Still in the house

Misperceptions

She follows her grandson
Down the mountain trail
Glances back
Sees a man
Thinks
No threat

A stallion grazing
Looks up
Charges

She's on the ground
Her body covering the boy
Certain they'll be trampled
She prays
God, please keep us from feeling
    the pain

Hooves surround, safe
Beneath the stallion.

Serpent Fire

Glistening scale-like skin
All green and blue metallic hues
Triangle head
Rising up
From a thick, coiled body.

The serpent fire
Coiled at the base of the spine
Rises upward
Transforming, healing
Bringing new dimensions
To Life.

Once upon a Time

Once upon a time
There was a little girl
Her name was
    Sandra
She struggled with life
Got what she never
    came for
Fear and loathing
Learned she was bad
That it was her fault
That nobody cared
That nobody came
Nobody helped
She had to fend for
    Herself
So she went inside
The world around her
    was
      too scary a place

Now
She's trying to come out

When there's no one
　　About
But me

I feel her pain
I feel her fear
　　Right here
In my body
In my mind

Burial Ground

Pieces of old scrap metal
Just beneath the grassy surface
Pushing up from their burial ground.

Nearby
    A new birth
        About to happen.

Naked

God, you've made me
   naked
Now dress me as you would.

The men say
"Only gray—
For success."

I see,
"Bright colors
For happiness."

Frozen

The Parkinson's took over
His body and mind.
All I ever told people was
My Dad had Parkinson's
And he couldn't work.
Never anything else.
That's how I defined him.
Perhaps, that's how I define myself.

His body became rigid
Frozen.
It took another's hand
To gently get it moving.
A body frozen,
A mind under
Lock and key.

I took that from my Dad.
Is this to always be my
Legacy?

Imprisoned inside myself
A cold, frozen body
A locked tight mind?

My Drug of Choice

Reading is like a drug
To me
It's like Lay's potato chips
You can't eat just one

I just want to sit
And read and read and read.
It takes me away.

2014

Open Mic

Open mic night
Names called
Poets perform
One at a time

I wait my turn
Heart pounding
Body shaking

I watch myself
Disappearing
See words falling away
Leaving my poetry
Looking like Swiss cheese
I have no written backup
Wouldn't help
If I did

I rub circles on my chest
Look inside
Calm myself

I return to my body
The words return with me

I hear my name
Walk up front
And perform my poetry
Friends and strangers clap

Back in my seat
My body shakes and shakes
And shakes
I rub circles on my chest
Look inside
And breathe
My body calms.

The Raven Comes

Oh, Raven
You flew in cawing
As I climbed onto the rock
To sit and soak in
The sun.

I sensed that you were calling to your mate.
I imagined calling to my mate
Though I know not who that may be.

But a calling out
        that I am
Readying
To welcome you.

Crow changed its tune.
Swallowing a new sound
As if taking in the essence of its mate.
I imagined my mate coming nearer and nearer
Each of us absorbing the essence of the other
        as we meet.

When Raven again took flight,
I imagined my mate and I
    taking flight
        together.

To Freedom

Oh, my soul
You've kept me alive here on this planet.
You wanted to stay, when I did not.
So…
I've worked hard to bring about change
Now…
Bring me the rest of the way
To Freedom

Sufficient?

Beautiful fluted bowl
Do you like holding
The jade
And the butterfly on a stick
Whose wings are spread in flight?
Or
Do you wish you were elsewhere
Serving another purpose
Living a different life?

Are you content
Where you sit
Never moving about?
Or
Do you wish for more excitement?

Is this enough
Just being
Where you are
Holding this space.

Do you know that
Your creamy delicateness

Filled with rich black soil
Holding the green baby jade
And the orange butterfly
Brings pleasure to my senses?

Life Stinks

Life is disgusting
Shrouded in mysteries
Wearing a face mask
Of the dead and dying
It's all gray
100% of the time
It smells like vermin
And tastes like ashes
It stinks to high heaven.

Pain

Pain comes
Unbidden
Not revealing its source
Bringing with it anger
Then sinks down
Hides awhile
Before showing its face
Again

My Muse and I

My Muse is elusive.
It sends out a poem or two or three
Then hides out for weeks on end.

My Muse is persnickety.
When I wish to write light-hearted, untroubled,
     carefree poetry
It produces only serious.

When I think to be still and write
My Muse resists
Insists on cleaning the kitchen or reading a book.

When I would toss out words
My Muse says, No!
Blocks the flow.

Wait.
Is that my Muse or…?
Do I have this all backward?

Is it me who hides out?
Is it me who is serious?

Is it me who reads and cleans?
And the Muse who would toss out words freely
    and openly?

What if I were to embrace my Muse?
What then?

Is it only the Muse that has something to say?
What about the child, the teen, the twenty-something
    and more?

What if they were to merge with the Muse?
What if I gave them free reign?

Would chaos ensue?
Would anything make sense?

What if I open the gate?
Will I drown in my own words?

Memories

I shoot them and,
Like ducks at a carnival,
They pop back up
Again

And others—
Poof, they're gone

Triggers

A single wild rose bush
Lush with pink blossoms
Takes me back
To another place and time.
A single wild rose bush
Lush with pink blossoms
At the edge of the path to the outhouse
Fills my senses with its wondrous scent.
But what lurks at the edges after dark
    That fills my body with fear?

Exposed

Exposed, exposed, exposed
Oh, the fear of being exposed.
What is so bad, I don't want
    others to see?
What is so terrible about
    me?
Exposed, exposed, exposed.
What does that mean
    to me?

Am I Crazy?

Am I crazy?
Am I stark-raving mad?
What would I find if I entered the darkest,
    deepest recesses of my mind?
Do I want to find out?
Do I have the courage to find out?
Will I just block the flow, again?

Relationships

Is it a relationship, or not
When one can't speak
And the other dominates?

Is it a relationship, or not
When one lives in fear
Of the other?

Is it a relationship, or not?

After the fact
After the leaving
When one hides out
Is that a relationship?

When one moves on
To the next in line
Can a relationship be
When one still cannot speak?

Where does that leave one?
No more partners.

No more pain.
So untrue.

How does one then
Heal from that pain?
How does one regain a confidence that never was?

Years upon years
Of isolation.

Years upon years
Of self-protecting.

Where does one begin
To trust?
Where does one go
From here?

In a workplace setting
In a poetry group
One friend at a time.
Reaching out to someone
One senses is okay
But certainly not
The other gender.

How does one begin to trust?
How does one begin to speak the truth
And unearth the lies?

How does one begin to live
Freely?

Dance

Two-stepping

Down the drive

Strolling back up

The San Antonio Stroll

Though I've never been to San Antonio

I love to dance

I've always loved

To dance

I don't dance

Nearly enough

The Discard

They discarded me
So I discarded me
Now I'm afraid to look
Afraid of what I'll see
In the discarded me.

I can see through the gray, now
It's become transparent.
I can see what's on the outside.
I'm afraid to step out
Afraid they'll see
The discarded me.

2015

I Am

I am
    I am
        The wind

I whisper
    And I howl
        And I cry
            And I scream

I am

I am
    I am
        The voice
            Of reason and pain and love

I am

I am
    I am
        The heart
            That beats
                In my chest

Filled with pain
    And fear
Longing for
    Love and peace

I am
    The wings
        Of my soul

I am me
    Longing
        To be free

Sadness

The hands on the clock
Slowly tic away
Tic, sad
Toc, sad
Round and round
Second by second
A never-ending
Cycle

Locked in its case
Behind its face
How to get out
How to escape
This endless
Slow pace

Alone in its shell
No one to tell
No voice
Except
The slow
Tic Toc

2016

Drive to Work

Driving to work
Reciting poetry
Singing
    "In the Garden"
And
    "How Great Thou Art."

Other times
    Repeating affirmations.

Driving cautiously
But no longer fearfully.
    In God's hands.

2017

Anger

Anger
Builds on itself
Grows and grows
Until the spigot
Bursts.

Then spews out
Like water
From a fireman's hose.
Douses
Sticks like glue
Blows away everything
In its path
Isolates

And the Breath

Guilt

Sits like an anvil
On my chest.
All the actions
I didn't take.
All the times
I didn't stand up.

Guilt

Comes in one
Color—gray
Gray like steel
Solid
Heavy
Duty not followed
Frozen
Unable to move, breathe
The breath doesn't come
Locked
Inside

The anvil
Shifts
The door
Cracks
And the breath
A trickle
of Grief.

2018

Brushing Teeth

I see shards flaking
From my teeth
Like the thousands of
Steel shards
Floating up out of my body
Midway through my
First shamanic healing
Leaving no trace.

Serenity

Sitting on a rock

Near the bank of the Crystal

Feet in the water

Moon rising, bright white

Creeping past a lone tall pine with dual peaks

Capped by ribbons of pink and gray clouds

That fade to gray

Above, Mt. Sopris, west face, red from the setting sun.

2019

Forgiveness

I forgive myself
For absorbing all the bad things
That were said to me.
After all
I was only a small child

I forgive myself for holding those beliefs for
        way too many years.

The woman has only just shown herself and I pushed
        her back down, because I didn't want to feel
        what I felt then and what I've felt most of my life—

The feeling that there's something wrong with me.

And now.
Now, I must let her out.
Look her in the eye.
And say,

It's time
It's time for you to come clean
It's time for me to forgive

To forgive me for believing
You.

For carrying this inside of me
Through childhood and teenage years
For carrying this inside of me
Through two abusive marriages
And thirty-plus years of being single

Buried so deep I couldn't
Access the core until
Now
It's so close to showing
Itself.
So close to setting me free.

And all I can do is say
    Thank you.
    I'm sorry.

Rewrite

In the park
Barefoot
Spinning
Counterclockwise
Time to go back and
Rewrite my life.

At the river
Feet in and out
Of the ice cold
Water
Washing away the old
Rewriting my past.

I am the mother
Dancing around the puddles
After the rain
With the 4-year-old me.

I am the mother
Cooking food
That nourishes the body
Of the 4-year-old me.

I am the mother
Wiping away the tears
Of the 4-year-old me.

I am the mother
Dancing in the rain
With the 4-year-old me.

2020

Early Morning

At the river
Doing my series of exercises

Spitting snow

Sun peaks out
Momentarily
Blinding me.

Gray again

After rain
Fresh air
Birdsong
Rushing river

Recalling
Hikes with Heidi
Stops to scan our bodies
And surroundings
Awareness time

Imagining

A blueberry pancake
Breakfast

Sun again
Glistening on water
Wet trees and grasses

Clouds moving on
More coming in

Something in me
Wants to stand tall
Feels expansive

I could live in one of these
Big, fancy houses

Why not me?

2021

Why Not Me?

I believed what they said

One piece of chicken for you
Others can have two

Others can express their emotions
But not you.

Don't sing and be happy
She might get angry

You do the work
He gets the reward

No prosperity for you
That's for others to enjoy

So, I locked myself away.

Now, I stepped through the gray
Saw the prison of my own making
Pushed out the walls
Put in French doors

Spread my arms wide
And set myself free

Free to satiate my hunger
Free to express my emotions
Free to laugh and play
Free to prosper
Free to pursue my dreams

Then, I stepped out the door
Into a world of possibilities

Acknowledgments

I learned so much of what goes into getting a book published from my friend and amazing publisher/editor, Marjorie DeLuca. Marjorie's expertise as an editor and in tasks I had not thought of such as layout, design, and all those things that made my book shine beyond writing the poetry.

What fun it was watching my friend and photographer extraordinaire, Barbara Reese, take photos for my book cover and chapter pages.

What Cameron Scott and Kim Nuzzo wrote for the back cover of my book brought tears to my eyes. They really captured the progression of my poems in ways that I could not have imagined.

It was enjoyable coming up with ideas for my book with my friend Judy Palmer, such as how to break up my poems into chapters, ideas on how to dress up the chapter pages, and general brainstorming. My friend Charlotte Bailey, another amazing poet, helped me address edits and revising some titles for some poems.

I must thank both Judy and Charlotte for ensuring that I kept the integrity of the journey intact throughout the editing process.

I also want to thank members of the Carbondale poetry group for providing a safe space to share and get feedback on my poetry. The core members of our group were Cameron Scott, Marjorie DeLuca, Kim Nuzzo, Barbara Reese, Patrick Curry, Tony Alcantara, Dave Teitler, and myself. Others came and went through the years.

Family, friends, and professionals have supported me through the ups and downs of my journey. It took the support of this amazing community of people throughout the country to help me prepare to break out of my chrysalis and finally take flight.

Sandra is a Minnesota transplant to Colorado
and the Roaring Fork Valley.
She is a mother of three, a grandmother of four,
and a great grandmother of two
who enjoys reading, writing and laughter
and is a lover of winter walks and summer hikes.

CPSIA information can be obtained
at www.ICGtesting.com
Printed in the USA
JSHW050509240421
13842JS00006B/14